Animal Architects

VICKY FRANCHINO

Children's Press®
An Imprint of Scholastic Inc.

Content Consultant
Dr. Stephen S. Ditchkoff
Professor of Wildlife Sciences
Auburn University
Auburn, Alabama

Library of Congress Cataloging-in-Publication Data
Franchino, Vicky, author.
 Animal architects / by Vicky Franchino.
    pages cm. — (True books)
 Summary: "Learn all about nature's most incredible architects, from what kind of structures they
construct to what kinds of materials they use to build." — Provided by publisher.
 ISBN 978-0-531-21547-0 (library binding : alk. paper) — ISBN 978-0-531-21584-5 (pbk. : alk.
paper)
1. Animals—Habitations—Juvenile literature. 2. Animal behavior—Juvenile literature. I. Title. II.
Series: True book.
 QL756.F73 2016
 591.56'4—dc23   2015000538

All rights reserved. Published in 2016 by Children's Press, an imprint of Scholastic Inc. Published
simultaneously in Canada. Printed in China 62
SCHOLASTIC, CHILDREN'S PRESS, A TRUE BOOK™, and associated logos are trademarks and/or
registered trademarks of Scholastic Inc.
1 2 3 4 5 6 7 8 9 10 R 25 24 23 22 21 20 19 18 17 16

**Front cover: A male baya weaver
building a nest in Singapore**

**Back cover: A beaver carrying
sticks to build a dam**

Find the Truth!

Everything you are about to read is true *except* for one of the sentences on this page.

Which one is **TRUE**?

T or F Some animals build separate sections to use as bathrooms in their homes.

T or F Animals only live on either water or land.

Find the answers in this book.

3

Contents

THE BIG TRUTH!

Beaver dam

Hermit crabs roll a
shell around to make
sure it is empty!

CHAPTER 1

Builders Big and Small

Foamy bubbles cling to the leaves of a water plant. But look closely: These bubbles are a nest! The male Siamese fighting fish gulps air and spits it out. The bubbles this creates float to the surface. After **mating** with a female, the male carries her eggs in his mouth and stores them in this fragile-looking home.

← A Siamese fighting fish's bubble nest can hold 100 to 500 eggs.

Why Do Animals Build Homes?

Animals build homes for many reasons. They use them to hide from their enemies. Their homes can also be a good place to store their food or to catch their next meal. Animals' homes may protect them from bad weather, the sun's heat, and the chill of winter or night. Animal parents might build or find a safe place for their babies.

A sticky spider's web is the perfect trap to catch food!

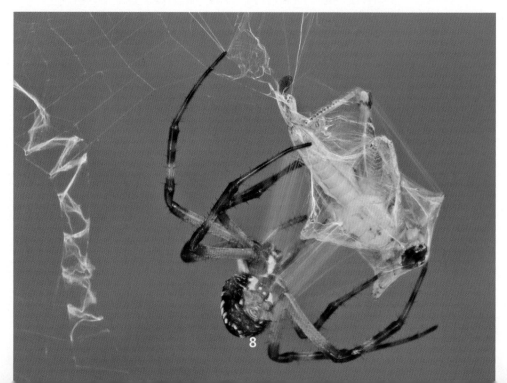

Muskrats often build their homes from cattails.

Building Materials

Animals are quite creative when it comes to building their homes. They use everything from grasses, leaves, and sticks to rocks, mud, and people's litter. Feathers and shredded bark keep the inside of an animal's home cozy and warm. The paradise riflebird even decorates its nest with discarded snakeskins! This might help protect it from **predators** who avoid snakes.

Some termite mounds are more than 70 years old!

Forever Homes

Some animal families will live in the same home for years. Many add on to a home that was built by their parents or grandparents. Badger dens are called setts. Several **generations** of badgers may use the same sett, adding on to the tunnel system over many years. In England, there are setts that are more than 100 years old. Termites also add on to their homes slowly, generation after generation.

Just Visiting

Some animals spend very little time in their home. Once an albatross learns to fly, it spends years living on the water. It returns to land only when it is time to lay an egg. Other animals' homes are only temporary. The hermit crab makes its home from the empty shell of another animal. When its body grows, the crab finds a bigger shell and leaves its old home behind.

Snail shells are a popular hermit crab home.

That Is Huge!

The size of an animal does not always match the size of its home. On the surface, an ant mound looks quite small, but underground it can be a different story. In Brazil, researchers poured tons of concrete into an ant mound to make a **cast**. They discovered a huge "city" that was equal to the ants building the Great Wall of China!

A small mound on top might hide a huge ant colony belowground.

Instinct or Learned?

Is an animal born knowing how to build its home? Or does it have to learn? Most animals probably use **instinct**. However, scientists believe there is some amount of learning, too. Animals have to learn the way back to their home when they are out gathering supplies to build with. Also, many animals must practice before they can build their home correctly. For example, zebra finches (below) learn from past mistakes and use better nest materials the next time they build.

CHAPTER 2

Above the Ground

What do squirrels, chimpanzees, and many insects and birds have in common? Their homes are built above the ground. Chimpanzees have open nests that are high up in the trees. This keeps them safe from predators. The chimpanzee's home is very simple, just a few bent-over branches lined with leaves. Chimpanzees know which trees will have the strongest, most comfortable branches.

A chimpanzee might make a new nest every night.

A squirrel's drey might look like it is just a pile of leaves.

Ready for Winter

Winter is coming, and it is time for squirrels to build their dreys, or nests. A sturdy branch in a sturdy tree protects the drey in strong winds. The squirrel builds a platform of twigs and then weaves in other sticks to make the walls and roof. Leaves help make up the outer shell. A hidden opening keeps the home safe. Grass and shredded bark make the inside warm and cozy.

Little Weaver

A tiny grass ball might look like a bird's nest, but it is actually home to a mouse. Both male and female harvest mice know how to weave a nest. First, the mouse uses its teeth to bend standing stalks of grass. Then it chews and tears other pieces of grass into long, thin strips. Finally, it weaves these in and out of the standing grass to make sturdy walls.

Only the female harvest mouse makes nests for the baby mice.

Fresh Air

Nobody likes a stuffy home, including termites! To fill their mounds with fresh air, termites use two things: tunnels and airholes. A network of tunnels keeps air moving into and out of the mound. Tiny airholes along the walls of the mound help, too. A termite mound works like an animal's lung with air whooshing in and out.

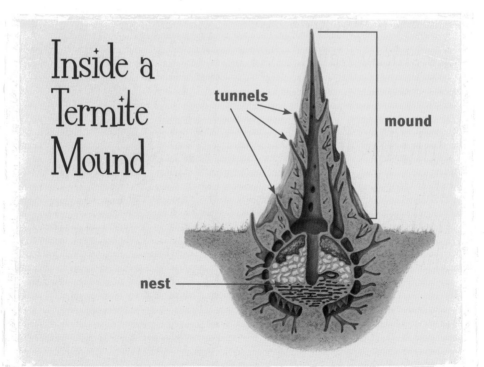

Inside a Termite Mound

tunnels

mound

nest

A wasp builds its nest cell by cell.

Building Blocks

Look at the homes of wasps, hornets, and bees. Although they might be made of different materials, they are all made up of tiny cells. Honeybees mold cells from wax. Hornets and some wasps make their cells from wood pulp. Other wasps use mud or clay. This cell structure is a very clever way to build. It is easy to add more cells, and together they make a sturdy home.

A group of weaver ants pulls leaves together to build a nest.

A completed weaver ant nest can be the size of a soccer ball.

Tailor-Made

You might know that ants work together to do many things. Weaver ants work together to sew a home! First, they find two leaves growing close together. Then worker ants carry a **larva** to this area. They squeeze the larva, and it makes a special thread. Workers attach this thread to one leaf, and then carry the larva and its thread to the other leaf. They "sew" their home together with this silky thread.

A Cozy "Oven" Home

Look closely at the ovenbird's home. Does it remind you of a covered pot? The female ovenbird builds her nest on the forest floor. Back and forth she weaves bark, leaves, and grasses to make a protective dome. Inside, she creates a sturdy "cup" and lines it with animal hair to cushion her eggs. Hiding the entrance on the side of the nest makes it harder for predators to spot her home.

An ovenbird works hard to hide her chicks in a nest.

The Borrower

It can be important to leave dead trees in a forest, because some animals make their homes there. For example, the titmouse likes the safety and warmth of a home inside a tree, but it cannot dig out a hole on its own. Instead, it borrows an existing hole that has been abandoned by a woodpecker or hollowed out by disease. The titmouse then uses bark, grass, moss, and leaves for its building materials inside the home.

A titmouse brings food into its nest to feed its hungry babies.

22

A mallee fowl adjusts the temperature of its nest by adding sand to it or digging holes in it.

Check the Temperature

Many bird mothers use heat from their body to help chicks develop. The mallee fowl uses heat from rotting plants! The male bird digs a pit and lines it with leaves and twigs. As this plant material rots, it creates heat. The male mallee checks the mound's temperature with its beak. When the mound is warm enough, the female lays her eggs. The father stays with the eggs and adjusts the temperature of the nest until the chicks hatch.

Body Features Help Them Build

When animals build, they don't use machine tools, cranes, or dump trucks. They have only their own feet, beaks, and teeth!

Beavers have a flat tail that helps them balance when they carry a heavy load. They also have sharp teeth that work like a chainsaw for cutting down trees.

24

Birds use their beaks to weave, sew, dig, and hammer.

Moles' claws face out to make digging easier.

Termites use their sawlike teeth to chew a home in a tree.

Some animals even make their own building materials. A bee's body produces the wax it needs to build its honeycomb.

CHAPTER 3

Hidden Underground

A prairie might look empty, but dig a little deeper! Below the ground is a prairie dog **colony** made up of hundreds of connected tunnels and rooms. The clever prairie dog includes back door escape routes in its rooms. It digs deep tunnels to avoid freezing and shallow tunnels to avoid floods. High mounds at the tunnels' main entrances keep water out. The mounds make good lookout points, too.

Some colonies are home to millions of prairie dogs!

Secondhand Homes

Many animals dig their own **burrows,** but meerkats are happy to let another animal do the work! They will often move into a spot that another animal has abandoned.

Meerkats usually live in a group of about 40 animals called a mob or a gang. Their homes have multiple entrances. This means that if a predator is nearby, meerkats have many ways to avoid it!

Meerkats often rotate among a number of homes.

Safe and Snug

Animals have homes that keep them safe and shelter them from the weather, just like people have. Some animals, such as squirrels, build their homes in trees, high above intruders. A layer of leaves and bark blocks the rain, while moss and feathers keep the inside of the homes warm. Other animals, like polar bears, make caves and burrows with hidden entrances and keep their babies safe inside. These homes protect the animals from heat, cold, and predators.

CHAPTER 4

Wet and Watery

Many animals make their homes either in or near the water. Some, such as fish, need water to breathe. Others, such as beavers, use water to protect themselves. The African gray tree frog builds a bubbly home for its young right over the water. The female makes a sticky fluid and kicks it into a bubbly mass. The female lays her eggs, male frogs fertilize them, and the babies develop inside the bubbles.

When the time is right, African gray tree frog tadpoles drop right into the water.

A beaver's dam creates a habitat for frogs, waterbirds, and many other animals.

Busy Beavers

Have you ever found a tree stump that looked like a sharpened pencil? That was a sign of beavers at work. First, the beaver packs logs, sticks, and lots of mud to make a permanent barrier in the water. This makes water flood the land, creating a safe place where the beaver can build. Next, the beaver selects a shallow area, where it builds a platform of mud. Then the beaver piles sticks, plants, and more mud on top, making two underwater entrances and a dry room inside.

Half-and-Half

Some animals live in water *and* on land. The female caddis fly lays her eggs in water. After hatching, each wormlike larva stays in the water and makes a protective tube of shells, stones, twigs, or leaves connected by sticky silk. The larva seals the ends of the tube and builds a cocoon inside. A few weeks later, once the larva has become a caddis, the caddis chews its way out of the cocoon, swims to the water's surface, splits its skin, and flies away.

A caddis fly larva builds a protective case using materials from its surroundings.

A Houseboat Home

Many birds build nests on land, but grebes usually prefer a spot on the water. From a distance, their nest looks like a floating pile of plants. The grebe builds a heap of decaying plants, lays its eggs inside, and adds more plants. The plants give off heat, which helps the eggs to **incubate**. Both males and females build the nest. They tuck it behind plants to keep their babies safe.

Hundreds of grebes might build nests on the same lake.

A male stickleback prepares its nest.

Attracting a Mate

For the male three-spined stickleback, building a home is all about finding a mate. The male gathers plants and seaweed and pushes them into a loose pile. He oozes special glue made by his kidneys and uses this to hold the nest together. The male coaxes a female into laying her eggs in his newly built nest. Then the female swims away. The male stays behind to care for the eggs.

Mound temperature determines if alligator embryos are male or female.

A Swampy Incubator

Rotting plants might not sound like a very nice place to call home. However, their heat creates the perfect temperature for baby alligators to develop. Before the mother alligator lays her eggs, she builds a mound of plants. First, she uses her sharp teeth to tear off plants. Then she uses her snout to push them into a nest. After laying her eggs, she covers them with more plants for warmth.

A Home for Others

This reef might look like one giant rock, but it is actually made up of millions of small skeletons. These skeletons were home to corals, tiny soft creatures with a sting like a jellyfish. Together, these skeletons make a reef that is home to thousands of plants and fish. A reef grows only about 1 inch (2.5 centimeters) each year. A large reef could take millions of years to build.

Coral skeletons are made of calcium carbonate, or limestone.

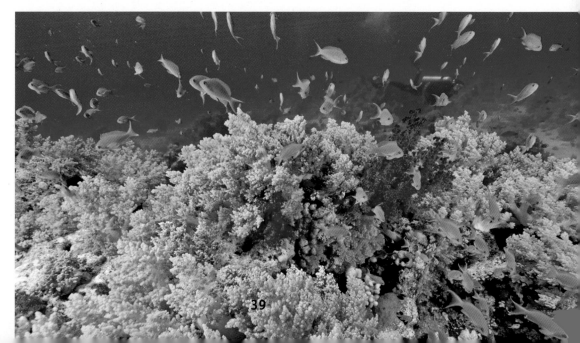

CHAPTER 5

Learning About Animal Homes

Animal homes are fascinating. Imagine being able to create such complicated structures without special tools, instructions, or a trip to the building supply store! Researchers watch animals in nature to learn how they build. These people may have to swim deep underwater, travel into dark tunnels, or climb high in the trees to watch animals in action.

 More than half of all black-browed albatrosses nest in the Falkland Islands.

Biomimicry

Has a building ever reminded you of an animal's home? The **architect** might have used biomimicry, which means copying something in nature. Some buildings look like an animal home. Others work like them. For example, animals can heat and cool their homes without electricity. Humans would like to learn from them. This would help solve issues in places that do not have reliable power. It would also reduce the use of fuels that produce **pollution**.

A shopping center in Zimbabwe was designed to imitate a termite mound.

A coral reef's colors come from the algae that grow on it.

Living Together

Humans are not always good about living in harmony with animals and their homes. Oil spills and divers damage fragile coral reefs. Prairie dog colonies are destroyed when ranchers attack them or prairies are turned into roads and buildings. Cutting down forests removes the trees many animals use for shelter.

Animals are important to the health of our planet. Let us work together to protect them and their homes. ★

Number of escape routes a meerkat builds into its burrow: About 70

Weight a weaver ant can carry: 100 times its body weight

Speed at which a beaver's teeth grow: 10 times faster than human fingernails

Height at which a chimpanzee builds its nest: Usually 33 to 66 ft. (10 to 20 m) up

Size of the biggest bird's nest built in a tree: Up to 9.5 ft. (3 m) wide, built by the bald eagle

Size of the smallest bird's nest built in a tree: About 0.5 in. (1.3 cm) wide, built by the vervain hummingbird

Did you find the truth?

T Some animals build separate sections to use as bathrooms in their homes.

F Animals only live on either water or land.

Resources

Books

George, Lynn. *Beavers: Dam Builders*. New York: PowerKids Press, 2011.

Spada, Ada. *Burrows, Nests & Lairs: Animal Architects*. New York: Lark Books, 2007.

Visit this Scholastic Web site for more information on animal architects:
★ www.factsfornow.scholastic.com
Enter the keywords **Animal Architects**

Important Words

architect (AHR-ki-tekt) — someone who designs buildings and supervises the way they are built

burrows (BUR-ohz) — tunnels or holes in the ground made or used as a home by an animal

cast (KAST) — an object formed by pouring soft or molten material into a mold

colony (KAH-luh-nee) — a large group of animals that live together

generations (jen-uh-RAY-shuhnz) — groups of animals born around the same time

incubate (ING-kyuh-bate) — to keep eggs warm before they hatch

instinct (IN-stingkt) — behavior that is natural rather than learned

larva (LAHR-vuh) — an insect at the stage of development between an egg and a pupa, when it looks like a worm

mating (MAYT-ing) — joining together to produce babies

pollution (puh-LOO-shuhn) — harmful materials that damage or contaminate the air, water, and soil, such as chemicals, gasoline exhaust, industrial waste, and excessive noise and light

predators (PREH-duh-turz) — animals that live by hunting other animals for food

Index

Page numbers in **bold** indicate illustrations.

About the Author

Vicky Franchino now has a much better appreciation for how clever animals are about protecting themselves from the elements and predators. Their homes are truly amazing! Franchino has written many books about animals and enjoys learning about them and sharing the fun facts she uncovers (just ask her family!). She lives in Madison, Wisconsin, and shares her home with her family and her yard with many animals.

Photo by Kat Franchino